Straight from the Horse's Mouth...

Straight from the Horse's Mouth...

And Other Animal Expressions

Teri Degler

Illustrated by Tina Holdcroft

An Owl Book
Henry Holt and Company
New York

Published in the United States by
Henry Holt and Company, Inc., 115 West 18th Street,
New York, New York 10011.

Library of Congress Cataloging-in-Publication Data
Degler, Teri.
Straight from the horse's mouth, and other animal expressions /
Teri Degler ; illustrated by Tina Holdcroft. — 1st American ed.
    p.   cm.
"An Owl book."
Bibliography: p.
ISBN 0-8050-0988-4 (pbk.)
1. English language—Terms and phrases.   2. Zoology—Nomenclature
(Popular)   3. English language—Etymology.   4. Figures of speech.
5. Animals—Folklore.   I. Title.
PE1583.D45   1989
422—dc20   89–31914
                                                           CIP

Henry Holt books are available at special discounts
for bulk purchases for sales promotions, premiums,
fund-raising, or educational use. Special editions
or book excerpts can also be created to specification.

For details contact:

Special Sales Director
Henry Holt and Company, Inc.
115 West 18th Street
New York, New York 10011

First American Edition

Printed in the United States of America
10 9 8 7 6 5 4 3 2 1

For Mom and Ken

Contents

Acknowledgments

Thanks are due to a great many people for their help with this book, especially my friends Paul Pond, Dale Pond, and Eileen Holland for the original brainstorming session that produced some three hundred "animal expressions"; Lew Gloin, *The Toronto Star*'s "Words" columnist, for his advice and suggestions; Suzanne Sherkin for her help with research; and Tina Holdcroft for her marvelous illustrations.

Introduction

Our furred and feathered friends have added a color, depth, and richness all their own to the English language. Literally hundreds of expressions and phrases have come to us from the world of animals: from their habits and characteristics, from the superstitions and folklore that surround them, and from the way humans have treated—and mistreated—them throughout the ages.

The way ants scurry and scramble about, for example, has given us the word *antsy*. When we use this slang term to describe someone who can't be still, we are actually making reference to the way he would act if he had *ants in his pants*.

The shape of the oyster shell gave us our word *ostracize*. It comes from the Greek word *ostrakon*, or oyster shell. In ancient Greece, crimes against the state were punished by exile. The vote that would determine the accused's guilt or innocence in such cases had to be taken by secret ballot, even though voting was customarily done by a simple show of hands. Since paper was scarce, the votes were marked on small pieces of tile, which were called ostrakon because they were shaped just like oyster shells. Thus, when we banish a person socially or ostracize him from our midst, we are, in essence, "oyster shelling" him.

An example of how animal lore has affected our language can be found in the word *cornucopia*. It comes from the Latin *cornu*, horn, and *copia*, abundance. The original cornucopia came from a goat owned by Amalthea, the daughter of the king of Crete. According to Greek myth, Amalthea used the milk from this goat to feed the infant Zeus. To repay Amalthea's kindness, Zeus later took one of the horns from the goat's head and gave it to her, saying that as long as she possessed the horn she would have everything she desired in abundance.

Rabbit punch is one of the terms that comes from our treatment of animals. We sometimes assume that it refers to the jabbing motions a rabbit can make with his front paws, but this is not the case. A rabbit punch is the quick chop someone in a fight makes to his opponent's neck—and it was exactly this kind of blow that was once used to kill rabbits.

There are a great many animal expressions that, at first glance, do not seem to have anything to do with animals. *Beat around the bush*, for example, goes back several centuries to the old European hunting tradition of sending out "beaters" to march before the hunters and, in a cautious, roundabout way, flail the underbrush to frighten the game out of hiding. Thus, today, when we tell someone to stop beating around the bush, we want him to come to the point, to stop being so circuitous.

When we say we'll have something *licked into*

shape in no time, we are harking back to the ancient belief that a newborn bear cub was a gross, formless lump of flesh, which its parents took turns licking until it was molded into the shape of a cub.

Incredible as it may seem, for several centuries this theory was held to be absolute fact by even the most well educated people. The reason the idea persisted for so long may well have been because bears keep their cubs well-hidden for the first month of life, and anyone unlucky enough to have found himself in the den with the mama bear and her perfectly formed newborn wouldn't have lived to tell the tale!

There are so many animal phrases and expressions that a book listing them all would become a small dictionary, so for this book, I have selected the phrases whose origins I found the most interesting—or surprising.

While this book is not meant to be a scholarly work, the information has been gathered from the traditional etymological—word history—sources and from the works of the contemporary experts in the field. In a subject as difficult to pin down as the history of words and phrases, however, the source books often disagree. In those cases, I have noted the fact in the text and have included either all the theories or simply the one that seemed most plausible.

It is my sincere hope that you will get as much

pleasure from reading this book as I did from writing it and that you will be left with an even deeper appreciation of animals and what they do for us.

As our world becomes more polluted and the opportunity to experience unspoiled nature is less and less a part of most people's daily lives, it seems to me that the animals we do come in contact with have even more to offer us. Whether it's the sleek beauty of a cat curled up on your lap, the uninhibited enthusiasm of a dog on a walk, the zestful chatter of a squirrel in the park, or the easy grace of a hawk as it glides above a nearby field, these creatures remind us every day of all that is good and natural in the world.

We should recognize how animals have enriched our language and our lives, and we should try to do at least as much for them as they have done for us.

Hounds and Horses

Dog Days

The ancient Romans called the hottest days of the summer *canicularus dies*, the days of the dog. According to their calculations, this period, with its sluggish days and sultry nights, started sometime between the third and eleventh of July, when Sirius, the Dog Star, would begin to rise each morning with the sun. The Romans believed that the heat from Sirius, the brightest star in the heavens, combined with the heat of the sun to bring about the unbearable temperatures. The dog days were also held to be the most unwholesome time of the year, as Sirius's influence was thought to cause pestilence and disease.

Later, people came to believe that this was the time of year when dogs were most likely to go mad, hence Noel Coward's wonderful and oft-quoted line that only "mad dogs and Englishmen go out in the mid-day sun."

Dog Eat Dog

We use the term *dog eat dog* today to refer to the ruthless competition often found in the business world. Unfortunately, it makes dogs sound like vicious creatures that go around eating their own kind.

In fact, the phrase originated as an allusion to the time-honored English proverb *dog does not eat dog*, which was another way of saying that there is honor among thieves. Thus, a dog-eat-dog world is much worse than the world of dogs, for in such a world, there are no holds barred and one cannot expect to find honor anywhere.

———— oOo ————

Dog in a Manger

A *dog in a manger* is a mean-spirited person who possesses something he cannot use or enjoy but refuses to let anyone else enjoy it either. The term, which has been in use for more than four hundred years, comes from one of Aesop's fables. In it a dog is looking for a place to have his afternoon nap. He spies an ox's manger filled with nice, clean, comfy-looking hay. The ox is nowhere to be seen, so he crawls in, makes himself cozy, and is soon fast asleep.

When the ox returns later in the day, he wants to eat some of his hay, but every time he approaches the manger, the dog begins to bark and snarl. The poor ox finally gives up and goes away lamenting how often people begrudge others what they can't enjoy themselves.

We have been using the phrase in English since the 1400s to refer to a person so mean-spirited that he keeps something from another or ruins another's fun even though his actions in no way benefit himself.

———— oOo ————

Hair of the Dog

When it's the-morning-after-the-night-before and a friend offers you a beer or a Bloody Mary and laughingly calls it *the hair of the dog that bit you*, or sometimes just *hair of the dog,* he is alluding— although he probably doesn't know it—to an ancient Latin medical tradition.

Since 1546, people have been using this expression just as we use it today: to refer to an alcoholic drink that is taken in the hope that it will cure a hangover. It came from the Roman cure for a dog bite, which was to pluck some hair from the back of the guilty dog, burn it, grind the ash with a mortar and pestle, and make it into a paste. The horrid stuff was then rubbed into the wound. The doctors of the day, it seems, based many of their treatments on the principle *simila similibus curantur,* like cures like.

I wouldn't be a bit surprised if the phrase *kill or cure* didn't arise out of the same tradition.

Hobby

In fifteenth century England, morris dances were an extremely popular part of pageants, festivals, and fairs. The dancers wore bells and costumes, many representing colorful stock characters. One of the most beloved of these characters was the Hobby-Horse. The dancer who played the part wore a costume made from a light wicker frame, which

Dog eat dog

was draped with colored cloth to resemble the shape of a horse. The character got its name from *hoby*, the Middle English word for a small- to medium-sized horse.

Eventually, a child's stick horse came to be called a hobbyhorse, and by the 1700s, people were said to be *riding a hobbyhorse* when they pursued an activity with the same tireless enthusiasm a child shows when riding a toy horse.

In this century, hobbyhorse was shortened in everyday speech to *hobby*, and the term came to be applied to any leisure-time activity pursued with childlike zeal.

———— oOo ————

Hobson's Choice

If you are offered *Hobson's choice*, you are being offered no choice whatsoever.

Thomas Hobson, who lived from about 1544 to 1631, owned the best livery stable in Cambridge, England. He was known to care for his horses extremely well.

In Hobson's day, most stables allowed paying customers to choose the horse they wanted to ride. This resulted in some horses getting too little exercise and in others getting too much. To ensure that none of his horses were overworked, Hobson rotated the order of the horses in the stalls, putting the freshest, most-rested one nearest the door and establishing a rule that each customer, as he came in, *had* to choose the first horse he came to. Thus, Hobson's customers had no choice at all.

Because the folks of Cambridge who could afford to hire fine horses were used to deciding exactly which horse they were going to be seen on, Hobson's rule caused considerable commotion.

Ultimately, however, his customers couldn't have been too unhappy with the results, for Hobson's business flourished, and eventually, his fine character got him written up in Thomas Fuller's *The Worthies of England*.

———— oOo ————

Horse of a Different Color

In Shakespeare's wonderful comedy *Twelfth Night*, the subplot centers around three characters: Sir Toby Belch, Sir Andrew Aguecheek, and Maria, who is maid to Sir Toby's niece, the countess Olivia. The three's antics, as they attempt to remove the arrogant and pretentious Malvolio from Olivia's favor, provide some of the finest low comedy in Shakespeare—and are responsible, in a roundabout way, for the popularity of the phrase *horse of a different color.*

In act 2, Maria mentions to Sir Toby that she can write in a hand very much like that of his pretty young niece. The moment she speaks, all three are inspired with a plot that will surely discredit Malvolio:

> Sir Toby: Excellent! I smell a device.
> Sir Andrew: I have't in my nose too.
> Sir Toby: He shall think, by the letters that thou wilt drop, that they come from my niece, and that she's in love with him.
> Maria: My purpose is, indeed, a horse of that color.
> Sir Andrew: And your horse now would make him an ass.
> Maria: Ass, I doubt not.
> Sir Andrew: O, 'twill be admirable!

Shakespeare wrote *Twelfth Night* in 1600, and within a year, the expression *a horse of a different color* was being used. It is possible, of course, that the phrase was actually in use before the comedy was written and that Shakespeare was making a play on it. Either way, we can give him credit for ensuring its popularity.

The phrase has been given another push towards immortality in this century in the film version of Frank Baum's *The Wizard of Oz.* When Dorothy first meets the munchkins and takes a tour of their city, she sees a horse that keeps changing colors. Amazed, she asks what it is. A munchkin replies that the animal is, of course, a horse of a different color. And so it is.

———— oOo ————

Horseshoes!

Horseshoes! has become a fairly popular way of expressing our sentiments when a person claims to have accomplished something through skill, but we believe it was really done by luck.

Horseshoes have been associated with luck for as long as horses have been wearing shoes. Before that, our ancestors actually hung skeletons of horses hooves around the house and barn to ward off evil spirits.

The belief in the magical property of the horseshoe is related, almost certainly, to its shape. It is reminiscent of a crescent moon—an ancient magical symbol—and to the U-shape of a bull's horns, a form that for thousands of years was believed to repel the evil eye. Later, the horseshoe became firmly established as a symbol of luck in Christian tradition through the legend of Saint Dunstan.

Dunstan, who lived in the tenth century, eventually became the Archbishop of Canterbury.

He was also renowned, however, for his crafts-
manship with gold and iron. A story evolved—
probably because of Dunstan's skill as a smith—that
the devil approached him one day and asked him to
shoe his hoof. Dunstan, being nobody's fool, recog-
nized his customer at once. He quickly grabbed
the devil's nose with a pair of red hot tongs, tossed a
rope around him, and tied him to a wall. Dunstan then
began to shoe the devil, intentionally putting the
fiend in such pain that he yowled for mercy.

In the end Dunstan let the devil go—but only on
the condition that he would never, ever enter a
dwelling where a horseshoe was hung. To this very
day, Saint Dunstan is depicted wearing pontifical
robes and carrying a pair of tongs in his right hand!

——— oOo ———

Hounded

Here's an interesting bit of trivia: Bloodhounds got
their name because they were the first type of dog
on which records of breeding—or bloodlines—
were kept. The genealogies of these dogs were first
recorded during the ninth century by the French
monks of Saint Hubert's Abbey.

Thus the "blood" in bloodhound has nothing to
do with the dog's ability to follow the scent of

blood. These dogs are noted for their keen sense of smell in general and their ability to hunt down any animal or person, whether bleeding or not.

Bloodhounds are also known for their tenaciousness during a pursuit; this is why we use *bloodhound* as slang for a detective or to describe figuratively a person who follows something up with pertinacity.

When we say we are being *hounded* by someone, we convey the same impression: it brings to mind the picture of a hound hot on the trail of its prey. The phrase is so apt, in fact, that it has been used in exactly this way for more than four centuries.

———— oOo ————

Mare's Nest

Today, we sometimes call a complicated, confused situation a *mare's nest*. The original expression, however, was *find a mare's nest*, which meant to make a discovery that in the end turned out to be no discovery at all.

The phrase was in use in this sense as early as 1619, and although it might not seem to make much sense to us nowadays, it was really a very straightforward kind of metaphor. No mare ever made a nest, so if you found one, you had discovered something that did not really exist or, at best, was not what it seemed to be.

One of the most infamous mare's nests in history was the discovery in the 1600s of an elephant in the moon by Sir Paul Neal, a noted English astronomer. Only after he had made a triumphant announcement about his discovery did he realize that the "elephant" was in fact a tiny baby mouse that had become trapped between two of the lenses in his telescope.

Can you imagine a more humiliating moment than the one in which he had to make that discovery public? Poor, poor Sir Paul.

——— oOo ———

Never Look a Gift Horse in the Mouth

See STRAIGHT FROM THE HORSE'S MOUTH

Straight from the Horse's Mouth

Modern day veterinarians will tell you what wily horse traders have known for centuries: that just about the only way to guess an adult horse's age is to pull open its mouth and take a good look at its teeth. Little by little, a horse's front teeth, or incisors, are ground down over the years by the daily chomping of grass and grain; thus, a horse whose teeth are still in good condition is estimated to be younger than one whose teeth are badly worn.

It is fairly certain that this method of trying to ascertain a horse's age accounts for the origin of the expression *never look a gift horse in the mouth*. The idea is that if you have received a windfall or if someone has given you a gift, you should not try to determine its value or look to find fault with it. After all, it was free.

It has also been speculated that this custom has given us the expression *straight from the horse's mouth*. I say speculated because even though the more traditional word historians offer this up as the most plausible explanation, they don't seem willing to make a very definite statement about it. This may well be because the explanation doesn't quite seem to fit: when we use this expression, we are not generally talking about having checked something out—as one would check out a horse's mouth—but about having had something said to us directly by a person who spoke with the voice of authority.

This, it seems to me, makes it worthwhile to consider that in the myths and legends of a vast number of cultures, horses not only speak, but speak with the voice of the greatest authority.

In one of the most all-pervasive of these traditions, horses warn their riders, who are often great heroes, of impending danger. Sometimes the horses are given the power of speech by the gods themselves. This particular motif appears not only in English ballads and Irish myths, but also in Russian, Lithuanian, Persian, Indian, and Cajun legends.

Horses that prophesy about other matters and that speak the hard-to-hear truth have appeared in other English and Irish legends and in a number of German, Greek, and African myths. In the Hindu tradition, Vishnu himself incarnates as the head of a horse. There is also a prophetic horse's head in Scandinavian folklore.

In his marvelous book *The Horse in Magic and Myth*, M. V. Howey writes: "In ancient days, when the gods made known their will and spoke to man by means of signs and auguries, the horse was esteemed as the medium of expression most favored by the deities, and so was an object of the greatest veneration and consulted in every crisis."

He reminds us that the great but corrupt emperor Caligula once spoke of raising his horse, Incitatus, to the office of the consulship, and he gives other examples from the legends and myths of the Persians, the Saxons, and the Greeks.

Indeed, it is in the tradition of the ancient Greeks that we come across the most poignant story of a horse that spoke with absolute authority. In the *Iliad*, Homer tells of Xanthus and Balius, two immortal steeds that were gifts from Neptune to Achilles's father. The animals were wondrously beautiful, with long drooping manes that flowed almost to the ground.

During the battle with Troy, Achilles loans the two horses to Patroclus to pull his chariot on the battlefield and bear him to safety. Through the intervention of the god Apollo, however, Patroclus is slain. Even though the horses could not have prevented his death, hot tears flow from their eyes when they realize their charioteer is fallen, and they rub their heads into the earth in shame, soiling their silken manes.

Later, Achilles, not knowing of their sorrow or their complete innocence, rebukes the two horses as he prepares to ride them back onto the battlefield. He admonishes them to be swift, to be mindful of the important burden they bear, and to pull him with greater care than they did Patroclus.

Straight from the horse's mouth

Upon hearing these words, Xanthus is overcome with emotion. He bows his head until his mane sweeps against the ground, and he trembles, for he is burdened with the foreknowledge that the gods have already decreed his beloved master's death. The goddess Juno, observing from on high, grants Xanthus the power of speech so that he may unburden his heart, and he cries out:

> "Yes, great Achilles, we this day again
> Will bear thee safely; but thy hour of doom
> Is nigh at hand; nor shall we cause thy death,
> But Heav'n's high will, and Fate's imperious
>   power.
> . . . .
> Our speed of foot may vie with Zephyr's
>   breeze,
> Deem'd swiftest of the winds; but thou art
>   doom'd
> To die, by force combin'd of god and man."

———— oOo ————

Yellow Dog Contract

In the early days of trade unions in America, workers were forced, as a condition of employment, to sign a contract binding them not to join a union. These were called *yellow dog contracts*, and although they have been illegal for quite some time, they were once a powerful tool in business's battle against the spread of organized labor.

The term became part of union jargon in about 1890, when the AFL and the Knights of Labor were first starting to show their strength. Before that, *yellow dog* had been an epithet for anything worthless, "low down," or no good. Yellow, when used in this way, meant cowardly, and there was nothing more useless—especially in the frontier days—than a dog with no guts.

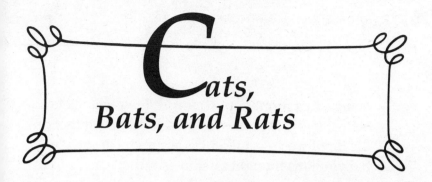

Cats, Bats, and Rats

Bats in the Belfry

We often say a person who acts odd or a little bit crazy is *batty* or *bats*. These are shortened forms of *bats in the belfry*, an expression that was coined in the late 1800s and made popular by Ambrose Bierce in 1901. He used the phrase in a story he wrote for *Cosmopolitan* magazine about a rather quaint minister who "was especially charmed by the expression 'bats in the belfry' and would indubitably substitute it for 'possessed of a devil'" in his sermons!

The expression itself is a reference to the way bats fly frantically from a church tower when the bells are rung. It is an analogy in which the belfry represents the head and bats the wild and disordered thoughts an insane person is believed to have.

It should come as no surprise that bats were associated with a condition the uneducated found as disturbing as insanity. Bats—with their furry bodies, leathery wings, fanged teeth, and rat-like faces—are bizarre creatures at best. They have long been the subject of superstition and strange folk beliefs. In a number of countries they were held to be evil spirits, witches' familiars, and even the form the devil was most likely to assume. The ancient Babylonians thought all ghosts turned themselves into bats so that they could fly through the evening sky. In some countries, people still believe that the ghosts of murdered men take the shape of bats in order to haunt their killers.

———— oOo ————

Bell the Cat

The use of the expression *bell the cat* can be traced back to the classic poem *Piers Plowman*. Written in the 1300s by William Langland, the poem is a scathing satire of Middle English society. It contains a story—probably borrowed from Aesop—about a group of mice who were being relentlessly pursued by the village cat.

The mice's friends and relatives were disappearing at an alarming rate, and they decided something had to be done. They called an emergency mouse-council meeting, where a number of ideas were discussed and rejected. Finally, one cunning old mouse suggested that a bell tied around the cat's neck would be the answer to all their problems as its tinkling would warn them of the cat's approach and give them all time to hide.

The mouse-council applauded the idea enthusi-astically and became quite carried away in their joy and relief—until one bright young fellow piped up, saying: "Yes, but who's to bell the cat?"

That put a damper on the celebration, just as it does today whenever it comes up in an office meeting, where it can generally be translated to mean: "Yes, but who's to ask the boss?"

———— oOo ————

Cat's Paw

When a person has been duped into doing some-thing unpleasant or dangerous for someone else, we say he has been made a *cat's paw*. The phrase comes from an ancient fable, often credited to Aesop.

A monkey and a cat lived with their master in a house. One day their master put some chestnuts on the fire to roast and left for awhile. The cat and the monkey were warming themselves on the hearth, and the delicious smell of the roasting nuts soon made the monkey very hungry. He wanted the chestnuts badly, but he was too smart to put his hand into the fire to get them. He gave the matter some thought and then began to flatter his friend the cat about his cleverness and bravery. In a short time, the monkey had convinced the cat to let him take ahold of his leg and use his paw to pull the chestnuts out of the fire.

Some versions of this fable even suggest that the little monkey not only succeeded in making a cat's paw of his friend, but also gobbled up all the chestnuts himself.

Oft-told tales like this are one reason why we have expressions like *monkeyshines* and *monkey business*, and why *monkey with* means to tamper with something or play a mischievous trick.

——— oOo ———

Fight Like Kilkenny Cats

Fight like Kilkenny cats is heard far more frequently in Great Britain than it is here. It means not just to fight with no holds barred, but to battle to the bitter end or until neither side has anything left to lose.

The phrase is said to have originated in Kilkenny, Ireland, where a troop of mercenary soldiers was garrisoned during the Irish rebellion of 1798. One idle afternoon, the mercenaries were amusing themselves by tying two cats' tails together, hanging them over a clothesline, and watching them fight.

A British officer heard the yowling and came to

put an end to the cruelty. One of the mercenaries saw him coming and quickly cut the animals down. By the time the officer arrived on the scene the cats were gone, but the bloody tails remained on the ground. Furious at what he saw, he demanded an explanation. He got it. The men told him that two local cats were fighting, and they were so ferocious they ate each other up—all but the tails.

I suppose the gentlemanly Brit was expecting a little too much if he thought that men who go to war for fun and profit would have much feeling for their furry friends.

———— oOo ————

Grin Like a Cheshire Cat

Even though the expression *grin like a Cheshire cat* was around at least a hundred years before *Alice in Wonderland* was written, Lewis Carroll gets the credit for making it popular. Who can ever forget Alice's amazement when she first discovers the grinning Cheshire cat in the tree and watches as it fades away until finally only its leering grin is left hanging among the leaves.

When Alice asks the Duchess why her cat grins like that, the reply, "It's a Cheshire cat . . . and that's why," leaves Alice as puzzled as ever.

The whole question, in fact, still puzzles people. No one knows for sure why Cheshire cats are said to grin—or exactly how the saying originated.

Cheshire was—and technically still is—what is known as a county Palatine. This meant the county was an earldom in its own right and, as such, enjoyed more independence from the crown than most areas in England. The witty folk of Cheshire were once fond of saying that this fact amused their cats and made them grin.

The most likely explanation for how this expression got started, however, is that the famous cheese from Cheshire, England, was once sold molded into a shape that looked like a grinning cat.

———— oOo ————

It's Raining Cats and Dogs

When we say *it's raining cats and dogs*, we are using an expression that has its roots in ancient super-stition and mythology.

Cats have long been associated with weather—especially bad weather. The Venerable Bede tells us that the sacrifice of black cats was common in Iceland, Norway, and the Scottish Highlands from

It's raining cats and dogs

pre-Christian times right through the Middle Ages. Those who took part in these strange rites believed that after the cats were killed and tortured, their bodies were taken over by evil spirits who brought on the savage storms common in those countries. By the 1500s the belief was widespread that witches kept cats as familiars, cats who were believed to be possessed by evil spirits—or at least to be "familiar" with the devil—and to love riding with the witches when they flew through howling storms.

Even today superstitions persist in various parts of the Western world that associate cats with foul weather: a cat with an erect tail is said to foretell rain; a spotted cat clawing a table leg is thought to be "scratching up a storm"; and anyone who makes an enemy of a cat is doomed to go to his grave in wind and rain.

Dogs came to be associated with storms, and particularly wind, through mythology. The Norse god Odin—or Woden—seems to have been, in his earliest form, the spirit god of the wind. Later he became the god of war and the dead. He was said to lead the Furious Host, a kind of raging army, through the heavens whenever there was a terrible storm. Odin, on these awful rides, was always accompanied by a pack of snarling, yelping hounds.

Thus, when we say it's raining cats and dogs,

we are harking back to the days when our ancestors believed that a storm was something far worse than a bit of nasty weather: it was a time when angry gods raged through the heavens, dreadful hags whipped along in the dark, and animals—possessed with magical powers and evil intentions—followed them about in fiendish glee.

———— oOo ————

Let the Cat Out of the Bag

Oddly enough, the expressions *let the cat out of the bag* and *pig in a poke* have the same origin.

Long ago in England, *poke* was the common name for a bag or sack. In those days, swindlers at county fairs would put a cat in a poke and, claiming it was a suckling pig, find someone who was simple enough to buy the "pig" without ever looking into the bag.

If the simpleton was not as simple as he seemed, however, he would grab the bag and open it before the swindler could stop him. As soon as he did, of course, the claustrophobic cat would jump out of the bag.

Let the cat out of the bag

Quiet as a Mouse

Quiet as a mouse is such a straightforward, self-explanatory expression that there is little to say about its origin. One of its earliest forms, though, was far more picturesque: *mum as a mouse in a cheese*.

There is also some interesting lore about what happens when mice are not quiet: It was once believed that the squeaking of mice, when heard at night, foretold the coming of a famine. If someone lying sick in bed heard a mouse squeal, it meant he would never recover from his illness. Finally, an old English superstition tells us that when you heard a mouse make a chirping, birdlike sound, it was a certain sign that someone you loved would soon die.

Let's hear it for quiet mice!

———— oOo ————

You Dirty Rat!

By 1815 *rat* had gained popular use as a verb that meant to desert one's political party or cause. This strange usage was based on the old sailors' superstition that rats would somehow know when a voyage was destined to end in disaster and would scurry off the ship just before she set sail.

Shakespeare alludes to this old folk belief in *The Tempest* when Prospero tells his beautiful daughter, Miranda, how they came to be stranded on a desert island after his treacherous brother had set them adrift in a very unseaworthy vessel:

> A rotten carcass of a boat, not rigg'd,
> Nor tackle, sail, nor mast; the very rats
> Instinctively had quit it: there they hoist us,
> To cry to the sea that roared to us . . . (I, ii)

Over the years there was a logical progression from its use as a verb meaning to desert to its use as an epithet for a traitor. By the early 1900s, *rat* was common underworld jargon for someone who ratted or "squealed" to the police.

These terms were once frequently heard in movies—*you dirty rat*, for example—and eventually they became part of schoolyard slang. After all, who—besides a criminal—is more concerned about being ratted on than a child.

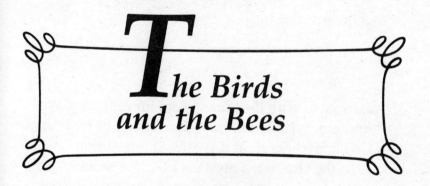

The Birds and the Bees

A Bee in Your Bonnet

People have been accusing each other of having bees in their heads since 1513. Not long after that, someone wrote, "Who so hath such bees as your maister in his head," a sentiment we are still expressing, four hundred years later, about our bosses.

You have *bees in your brain* and she's got *a bee in her bonnet* are a few of the other phrases we've used over the centuries to describe people who seem, as one nineteenth century word historian put it, "to be cranky, have an idiosyncrasy, to be full of devices, crotchets, fancies, inventions, and dreamy theories." Today, of course, we usually use the expression to refer to a person who seems obsessed with a particular idea or who behaves a little eccentrically.

There is a very good reason why bees have been featured in these sayings when we could just have easily been saying "he's got a hornet in his head" or "mosquitoes in his mind." Bees have been associated with the human soul for centuries. We find examples of this in various religious traditions, Greek mythology, and Western superstition.

To the Orphics, a mystical religious sect in ancient Greece that worshipped Orpheus, the bee was the symbol for the human soul because bees produce that wonderfully sweet substance, honey. It was also believed that bees swarming around their hives symbolized the way that human souls are drawn to the divinity. A Christian legend surrounding Saint John Chrysostom says that he was born with a swarm of bees around his mouth, symbolizing the sweetness of his preaching. In German folklore, the human soul frequently manifests itself in the form of a bumblebee. There is even a Siberian folk tradition in which the soul issues from the mouth of a sleeping person in the form of a bee.

Thus, when we say someone has a bee in his bonnet, implying that he is a bit mad, we are following in a time-honored tradition, for in the days before psychology became a science, madness was believed to be a disturbance not of the mind, but of the soul.

A bee in your bonnet

A Bird in the Hand is Worth Two in the Bush

This is one of the most popular proverbs of all time. It appears in scores of different languages, with only slightly different wordings. The Scots, for instance, say *better a fowl in the hand than two flying*. The Germans have *better a sparrow in the hand than a stork on the roof* and *one bird in hand is better than ten over the land*. In Hebrew, the idea is expressed as *one bird in the net is better than one hundred flying*.

In English, we once said *a byrde in hond ys better than three yn the woode*. But the most common version, *a bird in hand is worth two in the bush*, can be traced back to the *Idyls* of Theocritus. He used these words—in Greek, of course—in the third century B.C. when he was trying to sum up, as succinctly as possible, the same message found in two of Aesop's fables, "The Angler and the Little Fish" and "The Hawk and the Nightingale." In one, a fisherman keeps the small fish he has already caught rather than using it for bait in the hope of catching a bigger one. In the other, a nightingale tries to talk his captor, the hawk, into letting him go so that the hawk might catch a bigger bird. The hawk won't go for it, though: he figures the little bird he has in his talons will fill his belly much better than the big one flying overhead.

All this seems like indisputably good logic, until

you start listening to the philosophers on the more adventurous side of the fence who tell us *nothing ventured, nothing gained; use a sprat to catch a mackerel;* and *qui ne s'aventure, n'a ni cheval ni mule,* or *he who ventures nothing has neither horse nor mule.*

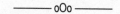

A Little Bird Told Me

A little bird told me is a saying we often use when we want to let on that we know something, but not how we found out. Although it is said in an offhand, lighthearted manner, it gives the impression that we have a secret—and perhaps not wholly benevolent—source of information.

It comes to us from Ecclesiastes:

> Curse not the king, no not in thy thought; and curse not the rich in thy bedchamber: for a bird of the air shall carry the voice, and that which hath wings shall tell the matter. (10:20)

Ecclesiastes is thought to have been written in the third century B.C. by a person whose pen name, at least, was Qoheleth. In the section of Ecclesiastes in which this quotation appears, Qoheleth is lamenting the political and social injustices he sees around him. This verse, in particular, protests

A little bird told me

against a government that you dare not criticize, for if you do, those in power will hear about it.

———— oOo ————

Crazy as a Loon

When we say someone is a loon or is acting loony, we are using a word with an interesting semantic history, one which provides us with a good example of how animals—and their character-istics—can affect our language.

The word *loony*, in the sense of being silly or demented, has been in use for about a century. In Roman mythology, Luna was the goddess of the moon and, as such, gave us words like *lunar* and *lunatic*. The word *lunatic* evolved, in fact, because it was long believed that madness was related to the phases of the moon. One very prevalent folk belief, for instance, was that sleeping with the light of the full moon on your face would make you insane.

From this, it would seem clear that our words *loon* and *loony* evolved directly—as alternate spellings from the root *luna*. This, however, is not strictly the case, for it is unlikely that either of these words would have carried enough impact to remain popular in everyday speech for so long if it had not been for the wild and crazy laughter of the loon.

To anyone with a little imagination, the cry of the loon at nightfall on a lonely lake sounds very much like the laugh of the proverbial madman. Indeed, this is the image that most of us have somewhere in the back of our minds when we use the word loony, especially when we tell someone, even in jest, that he belongs in a loony bin.

———— oOo ————

Eagle-eyed

The strength of the eagle's eyes is legendary. An American Indian tradition tells us that the eagle can see for a thousand miles. The bird's keen vision is also proclaimed in the Old Testament when the Lord speaks to Job about "the eagle who mounts up and makes his nest on high" in the rocky crags, and who from there can spy his prey with eyes that "behold it afar off."

Another ancient legend tells us that the eagle alone, of all birds, can look directly at the sun. It was even believed that eagles would test their young by making them stare into the sun. If a baby bird's eyes watered, it would be cast from the nest, for the parent eagles would know that it was not truly their own.

This is the belief Shakespeare was thinking of when he wrote that powerful line in act 2, scene 1 of

Henry VI, Part III, when the hunchback Richard cries out to his brother Edward, who also longs to be king:

> Nay, if thou be that princely eagle's bird,
> Show thy descent by gazing 'gainst the sun.

——— oOo ———

Eat Crow

During an armistice in the War of 1812, a young soldier from New England is said to have gone out hunting one day. He saw a crow fly overhead, fired a shot, and brought it down, unaware that he had crossed the enemy line. A British officer who happened to hear the shot and see the American decided that he would teach the trespasser a lesson, in spite of the fact that he himself had no gun.

He approached the Yankee in an open, friendly manner, praised his marksmanship for awhile, and then asked if he could take a look at the gun. The Yankee, seeing no reason why he shouldn't be civil during an armistice, handed over the gun.

As soon as he did he was sorry. The redcoat trained the gun on him, called him a trespasser, forced him to his knees, and made him tear a piece of the crow off with his teeth and eat it. As you can imagine, this riled the friendly New Englander right up, but he ate that piece of crow without saying a word and pretended to be very humble.

The redcoat finally decided that the boy had had enough and returned the gun. In an instant the tables were turned. The British officer was on the ground being forced to eat not one bite, but the whole crow.

The story spread quickly, and within a few decades, *eat crow* was being used just as it is today. The expression still seems particularly appropriate when it refers to an act of humility performed by someone who once—if only for a moment—held the upper hand.

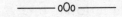

Feather in Your Cap

It is not uncommon around the office these days to hear someone say "that's a feather in your cap" when a fellow employee has accomplished something that is sure to make the boss sit up and take notice.

The expression comes from a custom common in cultures ranging from the ancient Lycian and Asian to the American Indian in which a warrior would put one bird feather in his headgear for every enemy he killed. It was once common—and still is in some parts of Europe—for the hunter who shot the first woodcock of the day to put one of its tail feathers in his hat.

There was a time in Hungary, however, when no one was allowed to wear a feather in his cap— unless, of course, he had killed a Turk.

——— oOo ———

Fly in the Ointment

The fly has been the symbol for something that is small or insignificant since very early times. A *fly in the ointment* is a trifling detail or seemingly insignificant person that spoils our enjoyment of an event or the success of a project.

The expression has been used in this sense since the 1800s, but it originally came from the Old Testament, where one of the maxims found listed in the tenth chapter of Ecclesiastes states that "dead flies make the perfumer's ointment give off an evil odor" and adds that "a little folly" can do the same to someone who has a reputation for wisdom and honor.

Truer words have probably never been spoken— just ask any small-town minister or politician who has ever been caught kicking up his heels!

Loony

See CRAZY AS A LOON

——— oOo ———

Make a Beeline

We all know that to *make a beeline* means to get somewhere by the shortest possible route. Most word historians agree that a beeline is the shortest distance between two points and that the term comes to us from the very direct path a bee is said to take when he is heading back to his hive.

I have it on the authority of a top-notch beekeeper, however, that a beeline is not the route the bees take when going home, but the one they take when flying *to* the source of the honey. The fascinating aspect of this is that all honey bees are able to make a beeline, for a distance of up to six miles, even if they have never been to those particular blossoms before.

How do the little buzzers do it? According to scientists who have been studying the phenomenon, scout bees are sent out from the hive to look for blossoms. When a scout finds what looks to be a potentially good source of honey—he knows enough not to get excited by a few scraggly flowers—he returns to the hive.

The moment he flies through the entrance, he lands and begins to do a little dance. The movements he makes are now believed to be a fairly complex form of communication that tell the honey bees exactly where the flowers are and precisely how to get there, for as soon as his dance is finished, the bees whose job it is to gather nectar leave the hive and fly, without hesitating, circling, or deviating in any way, directly to the blossoms.

Think about that next time you want to swat what you think of as a lowly little bee!

———— oOo ————

Sewing Bee

It seems that both the busyness of the bee and the spirit of cooperation he exhibits when he works with his brother bees were the inspiration for terms like *husking bee*, *sewing bee*, and *quilting bee*.

This type of activity, where neighbors come together to work on a common project and socialize at the same time, was common among the yeomanry of England as early as the Middle Ages. Yankees, however, get the credit for giving the "bee" its name and making it such a popular way to get work done.

The vast distances between homesteads in the Old West and the tremendous amount of heavy labor involved in making the land habitable were just two of the reasons why bees were so important in the pioneer way of life. If the pioneers didn't work together, certain jobs—like building schools for their children—simply wouldn't get done. As well, most people lived such isolated lives that just getting together with their neighbors was reason enough for having a celebration—after the work was done, of course.

Unfortunately, in some of the wilder parts of the frontier, the folks got a little over-inspired by the industry of the bee: they came up with the *tar and feather bee*, the *lynching bee*, and the *hanging bee*.

———— oOo ————

Swan Song

The last masterpiece a great writer, musician, or artist creates before his or her death is often called a *swan song*. This is an allusion to the ancient belief that swans keep silent for their entire lives and then, at the moment preceding death, burst into a glorious song.

There is also a Greek legend that tells us that the soul of Apollo, the god of music and poetry, passed into a swan at his death. Later, there was the Pythagorean idea that the souls of all great poets transmigrated to swans when they died. This was almost certainly the idea being alluded to when later writers came to call Shakespeare the Swan of Avon and Virgil the Swan of Mantua.

Scientists, of course, will tell you that swans do not sing at all and that, certainly, no swan ever caroled out joyfully just before it died. This is, nonetheless, exactly the kind of tale that romantics like to go right on believing. And why not? Plato, Aristotle, and Cicero all believed it to be true.

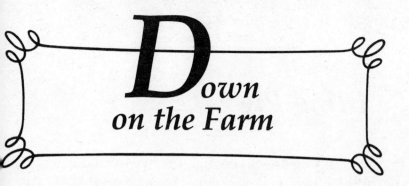

Down on the Farm

Adam's Off Ox

If you are from New England, you are probably familiar with this colorful expression. It's often used in sentences like "he didn't know me from Adam's off ox" and is usually said of a person who acts as if he is much more "buddy-buddy" with someone than he actually is.

An off ox is the ox on the right side of a team of oxen. He is called the off ox because he is the one who is farthest away from the driver. In some parts of the country, an uncoordinated person is sometimes said to be *as clumsy as an off ox*. This is because the team driver has less control over the ox on the right side, and it has, therefore, a greater tendency to stumble.

Just in case you're interested, the ox on the left side is called the near ox.

Blind Pig

Unless you are old enough to have lived during Prohibition, you may never have heard this unusual phrase. A *blind pig*—sometimes also called a *blind tiger*—was a place where alcohol was sold illicitly.

Interestingly enough, both terms were in use long before Prohibition began. There have always been areas of the United States where the sale of liquor was illegal, and as a result, there have always been illegal drinking establishments. These places were called blind pigs as early as 1840. Supposedly, folks who wanted to sell booze in a "dry" area would cut a hole in the side of a wall— perhaps in their barn—and cover it with a flap. Then, in true carnival fashion, they would hang up a sign that said "Blind Pig—10¢ a peep."

Those in the know would come by, slap down their dime, and demand a look-see. When the flap was drawn back, they got their kicks, not from a peek at a wild cat or deformed pig, but from a belt of good, strong whiskey—made all the tastier, of course, by the thrill of defying the law.

Bring Home the Bacon

Bring home the bacon may be a reference to the game, once popular at county fairs, of vying to catch a greased pig. The winner got to take the pig home and, if he so desired, turn the little squealer into bacon.

It seems more likely, however, that the saying arose from a custom that began in 1111 in Dunmow, Essex. A lady named Juga, a member of the nobility, felt strongly that marital happiness should be rewarded and said that she would award a flitch—meaning a whole side—of bacon to anyone who would come to Dunmow, kneel humbly on the two sharp stones that were near the church door, and swear before God that he had not had a family quarrel or wished that he had never married for at least twelve months and a day.

The practice of giving out the Dunmow flitch died out for a while, presumably after the noble Juga's death. It was reinstated, however, in 1244 by one Robert de Fitzwalter. The custom continued from 1244 until 1772, and in that entire time, 528 years, the prize was given out only eight times.

The names of the thrice-blessed folk who managed to bring home the bacon are recorded permanently at Dunmow, and they have thus achieved some degree of immortality. Deservedly so.

Bulldoze

See COME ON LIKE A BULLDOZER

——— oOo ———

Clumsy as an Off Ox

See ADAM'S OFF OX

——— oOo ———

Cock-and-Bull Story

We have been calling long, rambling, unbelievable tales *cock-and-bull stories* since at least 1608. The phrase probably originated as a reference to age-old, fabulous tales in which cocks, bulls, and other animals speak to each other—and to people—using human speech. There may even have been a fable, now lost, that was actually called "The Cock and the Bull."

The Cock and The Bull were also popular pub names in seventeenth-century England. Two so-named pubs once existed catercorner to each other in the town of Stony Stratford, Buckinghamshire. In the olden days, the coach from London to Birmingham changed horses at The Cock, and the coach from Birmingham to London did the same at The Bull. Because Stony Stratford is located almost exactly midway between the two cities, the stages usually arrived at about the same time. The more-talkative passengers, delighted at finding a new audience for their stories, would gather at one of the pubs and swap tall tales while they waited for their coaches to be readied.

Many word historians believe that this is where the phrase comes from; the people of Stony Stratford are, of course, quite certain.

——— oOo ———

Cock of the Walk

Cocky, cocksure, and *cock of the walk* all come from the feisty, confident way the barnyard rooster and his cousin, the game-cock, strut and swagger about their territory. The "walk" in *cock of the walk* is an old English term for the part of the barnyard where the fowls are fed. Because one cock will not allow another in the walk until they have battled for supremacy, we say a person thinks he is the cock of the walk when he is acting like he owns the world.

These expressions have been used just as we use

them today for hundreds of years. Long before that, the cock's pride and arrogance caused people to associate him with the gods. In Greek mythology, the cock, who announces the dawn, was considered sacred to Apollo, the sun god. The cock was sometimes called the Son of Mars because of his pugnaciousness and ability to fight. In ancient Mexico cocks were considered the most fitting animals to be sacrificed to the gods, and they were held in such high esteem that they could be substituted for humans in sacrificial rites.

Today, terms like cocky and cocksure are supposed to be derogatory, but they often cloak a grudging admiration. The cock has, after all, been a symbol of fertility and virility throughout Western history, so it should not be surprising that, even though we find cocky people obnoxious, we often find them a bit sexy, too.

Look at the phrases *cock your hat*, *cock your head*, *cock your nose*, and *cock-a-hoop*: they all refer to a kind of cheekiness we can't help but admire.

——— oOo ———

Cockpit

Originally, a *cockpit* was just what it sounds like: a pit dug in the ground for cockfighting. The "sport"

Cock of the walk

we consider so inhumane today was a favorite pastime of both the Greeks and Romans. Later, the Romans introduced it to Britain, where it was very popular. From the twelfth to the nineteenth centuries, British schoolboys celebrated Shrove Tuesday by holding cockfights. Henry VIII made cockfighting a royal sport and had a cockpit dug at Whitehall. Even the deeply religious King James I thought cockfighting a splendid diversion.

This cruel sport was made illegal in England in 1849. Until that time, cockpits were commonplace, and eventually the term came to be associated with any relatively small area where battles were fought. Belgium, for instance, came to be known as the cockpit of Europe because it was a central battleground in so many wars.

By the 1700s, the area on the old sailing ships that was near the rear hatchway and below the lower gun deck was being called the cockpit. When the ship was loaded, the cockpit was below the water line and was, therefore, a dark and gloomy place. Long and narrow, it was cramped and shut in by the overhead beams. Usually, it served as mess for the senior midshipmen and surgeons, but during battle, it was used as an operating room and was filled with wounded and dying men. It seems possible that both its low, cramped appearance the fact that it was the scene of such blood and carnage may have had some bearing on how the area came to be called the cockpit.

During World War I, fighter pilots gave the nickname "cockpit" to the cramped space from which they had to steer their planes and wage their battles. Now, of course, any part of a boat or plane where steering is done is called a cockpit.

Cocktail

There are literally scores of theories about how an alcoholic concoction came to be called a *cocktail*, but not one of them has anything to do with a rooster's rear feathers.

One idea is that the term originated in the days when cockfighting was still popular in England. Supposedly, a cock's courage was sometimes fired up before a fight by slipping him a mixture of stale beer, gin, herbs, and flour, which was called cockale.

Another possibility is that the French soldiers who were in England during the Revolution showed the locals how to mix a delicious drink from Bordeaux wine and a number of other ingredients. The concoction was called *coquetel*. The English may have corrupted this to *cock tail*, a word they were familiar with.

There is also a chance, though not a very good

one, that the word comes to us from an old Aztec legend. It is said that there was once a nobleman who had a beautiful daughter named Xochitl. He wanted very much for the emperor to choose the girl for his wife, so he mixed a powerful beverage from cactus juice and sent the girl off to the palace bearing it as a gift. The love potion—if that's what it was—seems to have worked, for the emperor fell in love with the girl, married her, and gave her name to the drink.

One of the most likely explanations, however, is that the term was coined by Antoine Peychaud, the inventor of Peychaud's Bitters. During the 1800s Antoine, a restaurateur in New Orleans, made drinks mixed from a number of different liquors. Tony served the wicked brew, which practically knocked his patrons out, in those little egg cups called *coquetier* in French. Wanting to give his drinks a special name, he simply Americanized the French word by changing it to cocktail.

———— oOo ————

Cocky

See COCK OF THE WALK

Come On Like a Bulldozer

When we talk about someone *coming on like a bulldozer*, we mean that their actions are far more threatening or intimidating than necessary. While we probably have a picture of an actual bulldozer in our minds when we use the phrase, its origins go back to a time long before the invention of the earth-moving machine and, in fact, make the expression even more appropriate than we might think.

To *bulldoze* once meant to give someone a sound beating—about the "dose" you would need to give a bull with a whip to make him do what you wanted. By the late 1800s, the word had evolved to mean to intimidate with the threat of violence. In the Wild West, very large revolvers—intimidating instruments indeed—were soon being called *bulldozers*.

Thus, overwhelming things and people were being called bulldozers long before 1925, when the bulldozer—as we know it—was invented.

Cook Your Goose

There are two very different stories about the origin of *cook your goose*. The first may be only a legend, but it has been around for centuries, and there could be a bit of truth to it. It concerns a village that was being besieged by an army during the Middle Ages. In spite of the attack, the villagers felt very secure and wanted to show their total disregard for the enemy troops, so instead of making a concerted effort to defend themselves, they obtained a long pole, attached a dead goose to it, and hung it out over the city wall.

Now the goose has been the symbol of silliness, stupidity, and futility since earliest times, and the sight of one dangling right in front of their faces so incensed the approaching men that they mustered their strength, scaled the city wall, and set the city afire, cooking the whole town and its goose as well.

The first historically documented use of the phrase, however, did not occur until 1851, when it appeared in a ballad sung in the streets of London that lampooned Pope Pius IX and a Catholic cardinal named Wiseman.

The Pope had made an arbitrary decree that the district of Westminster was—as it had been in the days before the Reformation—once again an official Catholic diocese. The Pope then went so far as to give Wiseman, who was living in exile, the title of Archbishop of Westminster.

The good Protestant folk had no intention of standing for such audacity! Anti-Catholic feeling grew to a fever pitch and culminated the following Guy Fawkes Day—November 5, 1815—in the Protestants marching en masse through the streets of London burning the Pope and Wiseman in effigy and singing:

> If they come here,
> We'll cook their goose
> The Pope and Cardinal Wiseman.

Their Protestant protestations were of little use, however, for Wiseman, in response to their actions, wrote his classic "Appeal to the Reason and Good Feelings of the English People," and found himself presiding over a Catholic assembly in London in less than a year.

——— oOo ———

Don't Throw Your Pearls Before Swine

This phrase, which warns us so graphically against giving that which is precious to those who cannot appreciate it, appears in the very earliest of popular English writings. Langland used it to good advantage in the 1300s in *Piers Plowman* when he wrote, "Noli mittere Margeri perles among hogges," which means, literally, "do not throw pearls among the hogs." In the days when Middle English was spoken, pearls were often called Margery-pearls or Margery-stones. The use of the word that has become the beautiful name Margery makes the contrast between the lovely opalescent stones and the mud beneath the hogs feet even greater, especially when Langland adds his next line: "They do but drivel there-on; draff [pig swill] is dearer to them than all the precious stones that in Paradise grow."

Those of you who are up on your New Testament studies, however, know that the saying originally comes to us not from *Piers Plowman* but from the Sermon on the Mount, where Jesus, after telling his followers not to be judgmental hypocrites, also reminds them:

> Give not that which is holy unto the dogs, neither cast your pearls before swine, lest they trample them under their feet, and turn again and rend you. (Matthew 7:6)

Now that is powerful language. No wonder the phrase has been part of our daily speech for more than a thousand years.

Don't throw your pearls before swine

Get Your Goat

The *Oxford English Dictionary* tells us that *get your goat* is an Americanism that means to irritate or annoy, but the great book won't commit itself on the expression's origin. The authors say the most likely source is the French *prendre le chevre*, which translates simply as to take the goat, but which the French use to refer to taking from a person who has nothing to give.

I, however, have it on good authority—the good authority being a highly respected retired professor of veterinary medicine—that *get your goat* comes from racetrack jargon. Goats, according to this expert, have a soothing effect on the highly strung thoroughbred; for this reason, it was once customary to put a goat in a fidgety horse's stall on the evening before a big race so that it would get a good night's sleep.

If some unscrupulous person wanted to make sure that the horse would not win, he would sneak into the stall in the dead of night, steal the goat, and leave the racehorse to fret the night away. In the morning, he would return the goat, and nobody would be the wiser.

The exhausted horse would most likely lose the race, and the thief would have succeeded in getting not just the horse's goat, but the goat of his trainer, his jockey, his owner—and every last person who had bet on him.

Go Whole Hog

There are two very plausible theories about the origin of *go whole hog*. The one that seems to me most likely to be correct is based, I'm sorry to say, on a Christian's ridicule of Islam.

William Cowper, a very popular English poet and rather fanatical Calvinist, wrote a poem in 1779 that lampooned the idea that Moslems are forbidden by Islamic law to eat certain—but not clearly defined—cuts of pork. The poem was part of his *The Love of the World; or Hypocrisy Uncovered*. In it, he asserted that when Moslem holy men tried to ascertain exactly which pieces of pork were forbidden, their arguments were based not on what the Prophet really meant, but on which parts they preferred to eat. Cowper wrote:

> But for one piece they thought it hard
> From the whole hog to be debarred
> And set their wit to work to find
> What joint the Prophet had in mind
> Thus conscience freed from every cog
> Mohammedans eat up the hog.

From this, it is easy to see how *go whole hog* could have become synonymous with acting without restraint. Cowper was one of the most widely read poets of his day, and it is unlikely that people questioned his facts before they quoted his barbs.

The other possible explanation for the expression's origin comes from the fact that *hog* has been a nickname for a shilling in England since the 1670s. This peculiar term seems to have come into use because there was once a small silver coin that had a picture of a pig stamped on it. Since a shilling was a considerable amount of money in those days, to spend the whole hog was indicative of a lack of restraint.

Regardless of how the phrase originated, it was made widely popular in the United States during Andrew Jackson's campaign for the presidency in 1828. Jackson was renowned for his determination, decisiveness, and ability to see projects—no matter how immense—through to the end. Supporters of Jackson came to be called whole-hoggers.

Advertising executives of today would, no doubt, not even allow a slogan like "go whole hog" out of the conference room. But in Jackson's day it was a resounding success. He was the first president to be elected through a direct appeal to the voters, and his election is generally considered a major turning point in the history of American democracy.

Like a Bull in a China Shop

Like a bull in a china shop is one of those phrases that says it all. You can easily imagine a bull being herded down a street in an old village. The bull, suddenly startled, accidentally crashes through the door of a china shop. Frightened by the enclosed space, he turns to go, but in doing so, he knocks over a shelf. The noise scares him even more, and he crashes deeper into the shop. Delicate pieces of china fly through the air, clatter to the ground, and are broken into a thousand bits by his heavy hooves. The poor bull panics and begins to crash up and down the aisles, wreaking destruction with every step, not pausing until the entire shop is smashed to smithereens.

This picture of utter destruction is also, according to one theory, the source of the expression *he doesn't have a chinaman's chance.* The person originally referred to here was not a native of China, but the owner of a store where china was sold.

When the English traders sailed to the Orient in the sixteenth century, they brought back an extremely delicate porcelain they called china. The stores where this porcelain was sold came to be called china shops and the men who owned them chinamen. A person with a chinaman's chance was someone who had about as much hope as a porcelain merchant who found a bull in his china shop.

"Hell" seems to have been added to the saying later, perhaps by Christians who believed that the Chinese were heathens, thus making it *a Chinaman's chance in hell*. If this was the origin of the phrase, however, it surely would have evolved as *he doesn't have a Chinaman's chance in heaven*.

With that assurance, I think we can safely give our friend the bull in the china shop credit for not one but two wonderful expressions.

———— oOo ————

Pig!

The hippies of the sixties probably thought they had come up with an original epithet when they started calling the police *pigs*, but they were actually using a term that had been around since the early 1800s.

In those days, of course, it was used only by the criminal element. London thieves gave the name to plainclothes officers who infiltrated their ranks and caught them red-handed at their crimes. No one seems to know exactly how this particular bit of underworld jargon got started, but perhaps it was an allusion to the fact the London bobby had doffed his usual spotless togs and donned dirty old clothes to "wallow" in the filthy streets with the riffraff.

It's more likely, though, that it was just an obvious insult. In fact, English-speaking people, in fits of anger, have been calling each other pigs for almost five centuries.

———— oOo ————

Pig in a Poke

See LET THE CAT OUT OF THE BAG

———— oOo ————

Pig Months

The months of the year that have an *r* in them— September, October, November, December, January, February, March, and April—were once called the *pig months*. These were the months in which a person could most safely eat fresh pork, for the months that have no *r* are all in the summer, and that, of course, was when pork was more likely to spoil.

Scapegoat

As part of the ancient rituals set down in Mosaic Law for the Day of Atonement, two goats were brought to the altar of the tabernacle. The high priest then cast lots, assigning one goat to the Lord and the other to Azazel—Azazel being the "desert demon" or the evil spirit of the wilderness.

The Lord's goat was sacrificed upon the altar. The goat named for Azazel, however, was left "alive before the Lord" (Leviticus 16,10). The high priest then made a confession, transferring the sins and transgressions of his people onto the goat. The goat was then led into the wilderness and allowed to go free as a symbol of the reconciliation of the people with their God. (Atonement, by-the-by, means literally *at-one-ment*, or to be at one with.)

For some reason, William Tyndale—the sixteenth century Christian translator of the Bible whose work was relied on so heavily for our King James Version—translated the words "the goat for Azazel" as "the scapegoat," probably because it was the one that was going to be allowed to escape.

The important thing about this goat, however, was not just that it was going to be set free, but that it was the one that bore the brunt of the people's sins. Thus, today a *scapegoat* is a person who takes the blame for someone else's crimes or mistakes.

Separate the Sheep from the Goats

Sheep have always received much better press than goats. Goats have been held to be everything from embodied witches to Satan himself. Sheep, on the other hand, were symbols of the good, the pure, and the innocent, probably for no better reason than that they have those adorable *sheepish* eyes and such soft and fluffy-looking fleece. Even the term *black sheep* underscores the idea that sheep in general are very, very good and that only the odd one out is bad.

In the Christian tradition, the very worst you ever hear about a sheep is the term *lost sheep*—a reference to the animal's tendency to stray—which is used as a symbol for the wayward soul. And even then the "shepherd" is urged to search diligently for his lost sheep and to welcome them with loving arms when they are brought back to the fold.

No saying reflects the symbolic difference between sheep and goats—or shows more clearly the raw deal goats have been getting—than *separate the sheep from the goats*. It comes from Matthew 25:32 and is a reference to the last judgment when the Son of Man will sit on his throne:

Before him will be gathered all the nations, and

he will separate them one from another as a shepherd separates the sheep from the goats.

The sheep, needless to say, go on to "inherit the kingdom," while the goats are cursed and sent "into the eternal fire prepared for the devil and his angels."

All this symbolism is well and good, but just for the record—and you can ask anyone from the sheep-grazing lands of Idaho, Wyoming, or Nevada—sheep are just as stubborn and perverse as goats. And they smell just as bad, if not worse.

———— oOo ————

That's a Bunch of Bull

If you're like me, you would probably bet any amount of money that the "bull" in *that's a bunch of bull* is nothing more than a genteel short form of what's better known as b.s.

But a bet like that would have lost you your money, for bull in this sense comes from *boule*, an Old French verb that meant to lie, especially to tell a very arrogant and boastful kind of lie. By the 1500s the word had made its way into English as *bull*, meaning to cheat or befool someone. By Dickens's day, a bull was an exceedingly boastful statement made by a person who was not aware that his facts were wrong. If you think about it, this is still almost exactly what we mean when we tell a friend that we think he is giving us a load of bull!

British soldiers get the credit for adding the Anglo Saxon expletive during World War II. They used *b.s.* to refer to the rules and regulations that called for unnecessary cleaning of equipment and excessive "spit and polish."

If you—like a lot of those British boys—come from farm country or have ever had the pleasure of cleaning out a barn, you won't have any trouble imagining why they associated the job of cleaning something that would soon be dirty again with our friend the bull.

———— oOo ————

You Old Goat!

You old goat is a particularly appropriate epithet for a person we might also call a dirty old man.

For literally thousands of years, the goat has been the symbol for sin, lust, and lechery. In Elizabethan times it was commonly believed that the devil sometimes took the shape of a goat and that even the average, ordinary barnyard goat disappeared at least once every twenty-four hours to descend into

Hades to have his cute little beard combed by Satan or one of his assistants.

The goat, innocent though he may be, is probably even responsible for those age-old representations of the devil that show him with horns, cloven hooves, and that sinister-looking pointed beard, which we call—what else?—a goatee!

Creatures that Slither and Swim

A Fine Kettle of Fish

A fine kettle of fish seems like it should be a lovely thing: trout with their rainbows glistening, salmon shimmering with pale reds and pinks, and bass gleaming a faint silvery blue, all laid out in a pan ready to be cooked and eaten.

Why then is a fine kettle of fish synonymous with mess, muddle, and confusion? The answer can be found in an age-old custom that was common in the southern part of Scotland. Each year when the salmon ran, folks would gather for a picnic feast near the river. The day's catch would be cleaned and tossed into a big black kettle filled with salt water and set up over an open fire.

Once the salmon was cooked, everyone would dig in, grabbing large hunks of the succulent pink meat and popping them into their mouths. Imagine the setting after about half an hour: a soot-blackened pot filled with floating fish heads and bones, surrounded by scores of boisterous people, all with mucky hands, juicy chins, and burnt tongues—a mess that could be caused by only a very fine kettle of fish indeed!

———— oOo ————

Chubby

When we call someone *chubby*, we are using another word that comes to us from the world of animals. The chub is a river fish that likes to hide in deep holes, particularly near the roots of trees. A member of the carp family, its coloring is dark green on the upper part of its body and silvery underneath. Its shape is—you guessed it—short and thick.

Very early on, the chub got a reputation for being a lazy fish, and by the 1500s, people who seemed spiritless, doltish, or foolish were being called *chubs*. The term was also used playfully among friends to mean fellow or chap.

The stubby appearance of the chub wasn't left out of the picture for long, however, and by the early 1600s, *chubby* was commonly used to describe someone who was short, thick, and dumpy like a chub. In the next century, the term took on a much more pleasant connotation and became associated with a sort of rosy, healthy well-roundedness.

Now, although chubby is still considered a fairly

polite way of commenting on that same state of "well-roundedness," in this age of the superfit and supertrim, the word has, sadly, fallen into disfavor once again.

——— oOo ———

Cry Crocodile Tears

Cry crocodile tears can be used in two subtly different ways: it can mean either to cry false tears or to feign weeping in order to trick someone. There are ancient folk beliefs about the crocodile that account for both these meanings.

According to one of these beliefs, the crocodile was the most hypocritical of all animals. He would eat a human being greedily, starting at the feet and working his way up to the head. He would then stop suddenly, look into the face of his victim, and being overcome with remorse, begin to sob sorrowfully over what he had done. Of course, once he had finished his little cry, he'd pop the head right into his mouth.

The other belief, which originated in ancient Greece and was taken seriously for centuries, was that the crocodile would trick his victims into coming within reach by moaning and groaning as if he were in great pain.

Cry crocodile tears

Sir John Hawkins, one of the foremost seamen of the sixteenth century, wrote the following in his log about one of the stops he made on a voyage in 1565:

> In the river we saw many crocodiles. His nature is ever, when he would have his prey, to cry and sobbe like a Christian body to provoke them to him, and then he snatcheth at them.

In all fairness to the croc, however, let us not forget that he was the supreme symbol of the deity for the ancient Egyptians. According to Plutarch, this was because the crocodile's eyes were covered with a thin membrane that allowed him to see without being seen and because he had no tongue, which showed that, god-like, he had no need to speak.

Drink Like a Fish

See LOADED TO THE GILLS

———— oOo ————

Happy as a Clam

Anyone who has ever heard the expression *happy as a clam* has probably wondered how on earth it ever got started. But hearing the expression as it originally stood—*happy as a clam at high tide*—clears the mystery right up, for even if you find it hard to give these little critters credit for any feelings at all, you have to admit they are probably happiest—as far as clam happiness goes—when they can't be picked. And they can't be picked when the tide is in.

———— oOo ————

Loaded to the Gills

We say a person who is drunk is *loaded to the gills* because—why else?—he has been *drinking like a fish.*
Both these expressions are very apt: A fish never

Loaded to the gills

stops "drinking" because he gets his oxygen by sucking water through his gills. Since gills are located just above the place where a fish's neck would be, if he had one, we have come to jokingly call the area under a person's chin his gills. Thus, someone who is loaded to the gills has drunk so much that he has filled his stomach—and every last inch of his throat—with drink.

——— oOo ———

Neither Fish nor Fowl nor Good Red Herring

During the Middle Ages, society was divided into three main classes besides the nobility, who were considered quite above it all. The first of the three was the clergy; the second included the general lay population—farmers, tradesmen, and the like; and the third consisted of the very poor—beggars, lepers, and urchins.

The people associated fish with the clergy because it was usually eaten on holy days and during fasts. Fowl was one of the mainstays of the common person's diet. But herring was thought to be fit only for the very poor. Thus, fish, fowl, and herring all represented clear-cut social categories.

When the expression became popular in the 1500s, something that was *neither fish nor fowl nor good red herring* was a person or an object that did not fit or could not be placed in the normal scheme of things. Today we use the phrase most frequently to refer to an idea that is so vague no one knows quite what to do with it.

———— oOo ————

Red Herring

It's a toss-up whether the British prefer to find their red herrings on their plates at breakfast or in their mystery novels at bedtime. When they eat them in the morning—though it's hard for me to believe that they really do—they are munching on herring that has been preserved not just by drying, but by salting and smoking as well. They call this ridiculously well-preserved tidbit a bloater!

When a *red herring* is found in a mystery novel, of course, it is in the form of a person or clue that cleverly keeps the reader from discovering the identity of the real criminal until the very end of the book. For some time now it has also been popular in business and politics to give the same name to a tactic that is being used to divert attention away from the main issue.

Originally, the saying was *draw a red herring across the path*, a practice that has been around as long as fox hunting has been a sport in England. It seems that a person who wanted to "fault the hounds"—in other words, to make it impossible for them to find the fox—could do the trick by dragging a bloater across the fox's trail. The smell of the herring was so overpowering that the dogs would lose the scent of their quarry and go running off in all directions.

———— oOo ————

Slippery as an Eel

Eels have been associated with all that is slimy from time immemorial. In ancient Greece, where it was believed that living things sprang forth spontaneously from inanimate matter, it was commonly held that eels created themselves out of mud.

The theory of spontaneous generation, amazing as it may seem, managed to stay around until well into the eighteenth century, and in the meantime, a number of other less-than-lovely theories about the "birth" of eels got started. One was that they came from putrefied matter; another was that they reproduced themselves out of their own saliva. The most persistent theory, however, was that baby eels came from horse hairs that had fallen into the water.

It was once believed that you could cure a man of drunkenness by skinning an eel and dipping the skin into his drink or—better yet—by floating a live eel right in his tankard!

Considering all this—along with the creature's slippery, slimy appearance—it's no wonder the eel has made its way into so many sayings that are used to describe sleazy people and unsavory doings. *All that breeds in the mud is not eels* was the fifteenth-century equivalent of calling someone a low-life. *Mud chokes no eels* was a seventeenth-century way of observing that a slimy person wouldn't balk at doing a slimy thing.

The phrase *slippery as an eel* has been in use since at least 1412, and the meaning hasn't changed at all over the years. Earlier in this century, *eel* was underworld jargon for a criminal who was too slippery for the police to catch, and several years ago, the term became a popular name for a politician who would never make a concrete statement. How very apt.

Use a Sprat to Catch a Mackerel

See A Bird in the Hand is Worth Two in the Bush

——— oOo ———

You Have to Kiss a Lot of Frogs to Find a Prince

You have to kiss a lot of frogs to find a prince has recently become a popular T-shirt and greeting-card message. It's quite a clever twist on an old theme.

Since childhood, we have all heard and read stories about princes who were turned into frogs— and frogs that were turned back into princes. These tales are actually part of what is called, by students of folklore, the beast-marriage cycle. It has appeared in a variety of guises in countless cultures, but the theme is always basically the same: A prince or very handsome young man is transformed by a curse into an amphibian or ugly beast. He remains in this horrible state until a beautiful maiden breaks the spell by kissing or marrying him—or some-times even by roughing him up a bit.

The classic tale of this type in western culture is a Grimm's fairy tale called *Iron Henry*. In it, the youngest of three princesses is playing in the palace garden one day and accidentally throws her golden ball into a well. A frog comes along and fetches the ball for her, but will give it back only if she promises to be his playmate and companion. He stresses that she must also share her table and her bed with him. The princess makes her promise and, of course, reneges as soon as she has her hands on the golden ball.

That night the frog shows up at the palace. The king, hearing the story, insists that his daughter live up to her word. The princess manages—with gritted teeth—to play and eat with the frog. But when she takes him to her room for the night and he tries—literally—to hop in bed with her, she loses her cool. She drags the poor little guy out of her bed and bashes him against the wall. Miraculously, what falls to the ground is not a splattered frog, but a handsome prince. She begs his forgiveness and, without further ado, keeps her promise.

Where does Iron Henry come into all this? He was the prince's faithful servant who, when the evil spell was cast upon the prince, had three iron bands forged around his heart to keep it from breaking. Even though Iron Henry is leagues away from the prince when the spell is broken, the iron bands snap off his heart, and they all live happily ever after.

Fields and Forests

Badger Game

The innocent badger had his name slurred in the 1920s with the advent of an underworld term, the *badger game*. This was a scam in which a blackmailer used a female accomplice to entice an innocent—innocent up to that point, anyway—man into a compromising situation.

At the worst moment imaginable, the blackmailer himself would slither out of the woodwork, camera in hand, and begin snapping pictures. The negatives would later be used to force the victim to pay the blackmailer.

The job was sometimes done so cleverly that the victim would never realize that the woman who had seduced him was in any way involved. She would then carry on her pretended affair, hoping to come up with new ways of bilking the bloke.

No one seems to know how our unfortunate friend the badger managed to get his name associated with this particular scam. Perhaps it's best not to speculate.

Bear and Bull Markets

The terms *bear* and *bull* have been common in stock exchange parlance since 1721, when a period of mad speculation caused the British market to take a terrible tumble.

A bear is a pessimist in the sense that he speculates that the market will fall. The name probably came from the expression *bearskin jobber*, which in turn came from the old proverb that warns you not to "sell the bear's skin before you have caught the bear."

This, of course, is exactly what a bear does. Believing that the value of a stock will soon go down, he contracts to sell a quantity of it—even though he does not yet possess it—to a buyer for delivery at a future date. If the value of the stock does fall, he makes money because he is able to obtain it for less than the buyer has already agreed to pay. If it doesn't, he takes a beating, for he still has to deliver the stock at the contracted price.

A bull, on the other hand, is an optimist. He believes the market will rise and makes his money—if he's right—by buying up quantities of stock at the current price and selling them at a higher price in the future. The term itself originated somewhat later than *bear* and probably came into being simply because an appropriate counterpart

Bear and bull market

was needed. And what symbol could have been more fitting than the animal who paws the ground, tosses his head, and charges his opponent, superbly confident that he is going to win?

———— oOo ————

Don't Badger Me

The badger is a pretty luckless creature all around. He is an ugly fellow with a broad back, stubby legs, and movements so ungainly that for hundreds of years, people believed his legs were shorter on one side than the other. He is doomed to spend his whole life burrowing in the ground—and he hasn't even been safe there since the Germans developed the equally short-legged little Dachshund that could follow him right down into his hole.

To top it all off, the badger gets himself featured in an expression—which stays popular for centuries—that makes him out to be a relentlessly annoying little pest. In truth, *don't badger me* comes not from the persecuting habits of the badger, but from the way he was once persecuted himself in a dreadful pastime called badger-baiting.

The sport—although we certainly wouldn't call it one today—was popular in England about two-and-a-half centuries ago. The lords and ladies of the day thought it entertaining to place a badger in a barrel and set hounds loose upon it. The crowds would look on, waiting for the moment when the badger—never realizing he was safe inside the barrel—would become so harassed by the barking and scratching of the hounds that he would run right into their midst.

The gentlemanly gentry would then call off the hounds and save the badger, only to put the poor little fellow back into the barrel again. This process would be repeated until the onlookers became bored with it and wandered away in search of more stimulating—and let us hope more humane—entertainment.

The original expression was *don't badger-bait me*, and it meant do not harass me again and again, in the same way that the badger was put repeatedly back in the barrel. The shortened form, don't badger me, was soon in use, and by 1759, *badger* was a standard English verb that meant to persecute one who cannot escape.

Once the sport of badger-baiting died out, people just naturally began to assume there must be something very nasty and persistent about the animal. Poor badger. When he wasn't being persecuted, he was being slandered!

Foxy

Students in the sixties would often describe an attractive woman as *foxy* or call her a *fox*. Feminism notwithstanding, men still describe attractive women as foxy—it's even used in popular songs.

Nonetheless, there is a fascinating and very ancient tradition that may well account for the association between the fox and an alluring female. In a number of European and Oriental legends, foxes are known as "shape-shifters." A shape-shifter is very much what it sounds like: a person or creature who can assume different shapes or forms.

In many of these tales, the fox takes the shape of a seductive maiden. The Western legends elaborate on the reason for this. They tell us that there were two ways of gaining the ability to shape-shift, a power that foxes were particularly interested in obtaining. The usual method involved studying the classics. According to the legends, a sufficient amount of learning would elevate the power of the mind to such a degree that the student would become able to transform the physical body. The greater the degree of learning, the longer the new shape could be assumed.

There are many European tales of hunters stumbling on a group of foxes sitting in a circle, one of them holding an open book and expounding on the classics. These foxes were said to be amazed that more humans didn't take advantage of all the opportunities for learning they had at hand and become shape-shifters themselves.

The foxes, however, sometimes grew tired of all that study. They would then choose to use the illicit method of obtaining these powers: sexual trickery! These sly foxes would study the classics until they could change themselves into a seductive woman for at least a brief period of time. While in this form, the "fox" would then seduce a young man—preferably a student of the classics himself—and would then use its powers to draw the life essence from him. The more human essence the fox was able to obtain, the longer it could keep the human form, and so the cycle went, until the fox was able to change into anything it wanted or to stay "human" as long as it liked.

Now there is no way to trace the word *foxy* as it was used in the sixties back to this ancient tradition. But then no one seems to know for sure who coined it. Perhaps it was a student of the classics . . .

Have a Monkey on Your Back

No one is certain how this expression came to be synonymous with heroin addiction. It may have been related to *have your monkey up*, a slang term popular around the turn of the century that meant to be riled or enraged. This seems to be a fairly likely explanation because when *have a monkey on your back* was first used, it referred not to addiction per se but to withdrawal symptoms.

The expression may have come into being because an addict feels weighed down or depressed when he needs drugs or because he carries, figuratively, such a terribly heavy burden. Monkeys have, in fact, long been associated with trouble. Before mortgages were so common, for example, the unfortunate person who had to carry one was said to have a *monkey on his house*.

—— oOo ——

It's a Bear!

Not long ago, it was common for students, when talking about a particularly difficult exam, to say *it was a bear.* The meaning was obvious: the hunger, ferociousness, and power of the bear are legendary.

Over the centuries, these characteristics have been reflected in many sayings. To *play the bear* meant to inflict wanton damage or, at best, to act like a savage. To *have a bear by the tail* was once as common as to *have a tiger by the tail*, and it meant the same thing: to be in a situation where there are no options but bad ones—if you don't let go, you can't get away, and if you do let go, the bear will be able to get you. *Savage as a bear with a sore head* is another expression that has been around for centuries.

The nature of the bear has even given us some excellent proverbs, such as "he who shares his honey with a bear has the least part of it" and "always call a bear uncle until you are safe across the bridge."

There are other cultures, of course, that have held the bear in great esteem and, in some cases, have seen him as something much more than just an animal. In the mythology of the Ute Indians, the tribe is said to have descended from bears, which are thought to be magical, telepathic creatures. Many tribal groups in the Far North consider bears to be immortal and will only hunt them when it is necessary for survival. Even then, strict ceremonies must be performed.

All this makes it very interesting that our phrase

it's a bear!, which now refers to something dreadful, was at one time applied by students only to the very best of things. In the slang of 1910, a *bear* was something exceptional or first rate—a real humdinger. A popular song in 1915 went:

> Everybody's doing it
> Doing what?
> The turkey trot!
> Ah my honey, honey
> I declare
> It's a bear,
> It's a bear,
> It's a bear!

——— oOo ———

Keep the Wolf from the Door

A concerted effort has been made lately by a number of biologists and animal lovers to clean up the wolf's badly tarnished reputation. But they haven't begun to make a dent: most people still think of the wolf as the most vicious of all mammals.

Just look at a few of the ways we use *wolf*: *werewolf, wolf in sheep's clothing, wolf it down, he's a wolf*, and *throw to the wolves*. Not a happy thought in the lot. And no wonder. In everything from Aesop to the New Testament and Shakespeare, the wolf is used as a symbol for ferocity, cruelty, greed, and especially, rapaciousness.

This all-consuming hunger is, in fact, what the "wolf" represents in the old saying *keep the wolf from the door*. When we use these words today, we are usually talking about keeping poverty in general away, but originally it meant, quite literally, to keep the spectre of starvation away from the home, for people knew that their bodies could be consumed by hunger just as surely as the wolf consumes his prey.

———— oOo ————

Like the Bear and the Tea Kettle

A person who hurts himself during a senseless rage was once commonly said to be *like the bear and the tea kettle*. The expression comes from an old folktale about a bear who lived in Kamchatka, a bleak, bitterly cold province in the most easterly part of Russia.

The bear wandered into a village one day and,

enticed by the smell of food, ventured through the door of a tiny hut. There he saw a kettle bubbling on the fire. Intrigued, he bent over and gave it a good sniff. Not realizing that it was hot, he got too close and burnt his nose. The pain threw him into such a rage that he wanted to destroy the tea kettle. With his massive paws, he ripped it apart and crushed it against his chest, burning himself even more terribly with the scalding liquid. The poor bear then howled so piteously that the villagers were forced to put him out of his misery.

Now that's a story with a moral!

——— oOo ———

Leonine Contract

See LION'S SHARE

——— oOo ———

Lion's Share

This is a phrase that is frequently heard in marketing circles these days, often in the context of a question about whether a competitor has any hopes of snaring *the lion's share* of the market.

In use since the 1700s, the term has its origins in one of Aesop's fables, the tale of a wolf, a jackal, and a fox who went hunting one day with a lion. After hours of effort, they tracked down a stag. As soon as it was killed, the animals began to discuss how it should be divided. The lion immediately took charge of the situation, roaring out that, first, the stag must be skinned and quartered. The others did as they were bid without question, thinking that they were each to get a piece. But once the job was done, the lion planted himself in front of the venison and made a pronouncement on the division of the spoils:

> "The first quarter," he said, "is for me in my capacity as King of the Beasts; the second is mine as arbiter; another share comes to me for my part in the chase; and, as for the forth quarter, well, as for that, I should like to see which of you will lay a paw upon it."

Thus, the lion's share is not just more than half of whatever is being divided; it is all of it—a thought to make a marketing team's blood run cold, unless, of course, the firm they're plumping for is the lion.

With this in mind, it is interesting to note that this fable is also the source of the British term *leonine contract*, an agreement that favors one of the two parties involved to the point of being ludicrous.

Lucky Rabbit's Foot

If you are at all superstitious, you probably believe that a rabbit's foot is a lucky talisman, but you may not know why.

It is the whole rabbit that is lucky, it seems, not just its foot. The reason for this, according to folk tradition, is that baby rabbits are born with their eyes open. Thus, they are able to see the Evil Eye from the moment of their birth and can never be cursed by it. The positive power of the rabbit is

believed to be so great that carrying even a small piece of one will keep a person from harm. Unfortunately, in actual fact, only hares—not rabbits—are born with their eyes open.

——— oOo ———

Mad as a March Hare

There is a theory that March is the mating season for hares and that this is why they are wilder in

Mad as a March hare

March than at any other time of the year. But isn't it true that these little critters mate all year long? Aren't they famous for it?

That being the case, the theory that the phrase was originally *mad as a marsh hare* seems likely to be correct. In fact, Erasmus explained the expression that way in the collection of aphorisms he produced in 1500. He wrote that the hares that live in marshes are wilder than other hares because there are fewer hedges and less clover for them to hide in. This, presumably, makes them nervous.

Regardless of exactly what it means or how it came about, it is one of the many expressions that have been made an enduring part of our language by Lewis Carroll. In *Alice in Wonderland*, the Cheshire Cat tells Alice she can further her adventures by going to visit the Hatter or the March Hare. "Visit either you like," he says. "They're both mad."

"I've seen hatters before," Alice decides. "The March Hare will be much the most interesting, and perhaps as this is May it won't be raving mad—at least not so mad as it was in March."

Monkeyshines

See CAT'S PAW

———— oOo ————

Play Possum

To *play possum*—meaning to pretend to be asleep or, in more critical situations, dead—is based on the possum's ability to feign death to trick a predator into leaving it alone.

Possums live mainly in the trees, where foxes, wolves, and dogs can't get them. But if they are foolish enough to be caught on the ground by a predator, they will fall over and lie in absolute stillness, even while the other animal sniffs, pokes, and prods them. The thought they hold in their little possum minds—which gives them hope while all this is going on—is that most carnivores like to kill their prey themselves and will not eat dead meat found lying on the ground.

Let's hope, for the possum's sake, that this is true.

Pop Goes the Weasel

Remember playing with your jack-in-the-box when you were young? You cranked the handle and it played a tune, usually "Pop Goes The Weasel."

While children today usually sing a little ditty about going round and round the mulberry bush, the original words were:

> Every night when I come home
> The monkey's on the table
> I take a stick and knock him off
> Pop goes the weasel!

The words don't seem to make much sense, and certainly, hitting monkeys with sticks is not the kind of behavior today's parents want to encourage in their children. This is another one of those nursery rhymes that means something quite different than it seems to and that had rather sordid beginnings.

Another verse of the original song went:

> Up and down the City Road
> In and out The Eagle
> That's the way the money goes
> Pop goes the weasel!

The Eagle was an old London music hall that was located on City Road. It was a particularly popular spot among the working class for singing and drinking. This clearly explains the line "that's the way the money goes." And as early as 1785, the word *pop* was common slang for pawn. Thus, when the money went, the hearty drinker pawned his *weasel*, a common nickname in those days for either a tailor's iron or a certain tool used by hatters. All this has led to the assumption that the original "monkey on the table" was nothing more than a figment of some poor stiff's delirium tremens.

———— oOo ————

Savage as a Bear with a Sore Head

See IT'S A BEAR!

Sly as a Fox

The fox has symbolized craftiness since earliest times. In Aesop's fables, the fox is frequently pictured as sly and full of tricks. Aesop's tales being what they are, however, those animals that use their common sense usually get the better of the fox.

In the Middle Ages, though, the crafty fox came into his own. He was featured in a number of different French, Dutch, and German epic poems as the character Reynard the Fox. These poems are all allegories; Reynard is used as a symbol for the Church and the abuses that were rampant in it in those days.

Reynard is a wily creature who uses trickery to accomplish his purposes, and he almost always manages to get his own way. The tales he stars in satirize such things as the Church's accumulation of wealth and the gluttony of the clergy; they also poke fun at people like knights and lawyers. These story-poems were written—actually, they were more often told—for the amusement of the lower and middle classes and were popular in different forms for a span of more than four centuries.

Between the ubiquitous influence of Aesop and the longevity of Reynard, it is easy to see why the image of the fox as a sneaky fellow is so basic to us and why sayings like *sly as a fox, crafty as a fox,* and today, *dumb like a fox* are so very commonplace in our language.

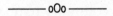

Weasel Out

Weasel has been underworld jargon for an informer since the 1920s, and *weasel out,* meaning to back out of a commitment for less-than-honorable reasons, has been in use for some time.

Weasel it out, in the sense of "I bet you can weasel it out of him if you try," has become contemporary slang for being able to get something—usually information—from a person by flattering or cajoling him. These phrases all seem to be references to the alleged sneakiness and cunning of the weasel—especially when trying to break into a hen house.

Weasels are also supposed to be able to suck the contents out of an egg and leave the shell empty. This belief gave rise to the really marvelous term *weasel words,* which was coined by a Stewart Chaplin in 1900. Weasel words, he wrote, are words that "suck the life out of the words next to them, just as a weasel sucks the eggs and leaves the shell."

The term was picked up and made famous by Teddy Roosevelt. In criticizing a phrase that had been created by Woodrow Wilson, "universal voluntary training," Teddy pointed out that "when you use the word voluntary to qualify the word universal you are using a weasel word; it has sucked all the meaning out of universal."

If Teddy was offended by "universal voluntary training," imagine how horrified he'd be by the political speeches and government brochures of today: weasel words galore.

———— oOo ————

White Elephant

Long ago in Siam, now called Thailand, the rare albino elephant was a highly venerated animal. All the kings of Siam kept these animals, and the highest title a king could bear was King of the White Elephants.

Our use of the term *white elephant* to mean a burdensome, costly possession comes from the story that the kings of Siam were known to occasionally give one away as a gift—but only to a courtier who had made himself particularly obnoxious.

The white elephant, you see, would soon be his ruin. The cost of its food and keep would take every penny he had. He could not return it to the king because that would be a deadly insult. He could not put it out to earn its keep, for white elephants were far too highly honored to be allowed to work as beasts of burden. He would never find anyone willing to take it off his hands, and he certainly could not do away with it.

Thus, when government critics call half-finished, billion-dollar projects that are obsolete before they are done *white elephants*, they couldn't be using a more appropriate term.

Bibliography

Brewer's Dictionary of Phrase and Fable by Dr. Ebenezer Cobham Brewer, revised and edited by Ivor H. Evans, Harper and Row, New York, 1981.

Dictionary of American Slang by Harold Wentworth and Stuart Flexner, Thomas Y. Crowell Company, New York, 1975.

A Dictionary of Slang and Unconventional Usage, fifth edition, by Eric Partridge, edited by Paul Peale, Routledge & Kegan Paul, London, England, 1961.

Dictionary of Word and Phrase Origins by William and Mary Morris, Harper and Row, New York, 1962.

Encyclopedia of Superstitions, Folklore, and the Occult Sciences of the World, vols. 1-3, by Cora Linn Daniels and C.M. Stevans, Gale Research Company, Detroit, 1971.

Folk-lore and Fable: Aesop, Grimm and Anderson, Harvard Classics, Collier and Son, New York, 1937.

The Oxford Dictionary of English Proverbs, third edition, edited by F.P. Wilson and William George Smith, Clarendon Press, Oxford, 1970.

The Oxford English Dictionary, vols. 1-12, Supplements, edited by James Murray et al., Clarendon Press, Oxford, 1933, 1972, 1976, 1982, 1986.

Standard Dictionary of Folklore, Mythology and Legend, vols. 1 and 2, edited by Maria Leach, Funk & Wagnalls Co., New York, 1949, 1950.

Take Warning! A Book of Superstitions by Jane Sarnoff and Reynold Ruffins, Charles Scribner and Sons, New York, 1978.

To Coin a Phrase: A Dictionary of Origins by Edwin Radford, Hutchinson of London, London, rev. 1973.

Zoo of the Gods: Animals in Myth, Legend and Fable by Anthony S. Mercatante, Harper and Row, New York, 1974.

About the Author

Teri Degler was raised in Idaho, but has lived in Toronto, where she works as a writer and editor, since 1974. Her first book, a study of positive methods of disciplining children with behavioral problems, came about as a result of her extensive work with young people.

In *Straight from the Horse's Mouth . . . And Other Animal Expressions*, which describes the fascinating origins of common animal expressions, Degler

KEN FAUGHT, TORONTO

indulges her fascination with words. That interest in words and her life-long love of sailing are also reflected in *Scuttlebutt . . . And Other Expressions of Nautical Origin*, the companion volume to *Straight from the Horse's Mouth*, which explores the origins of everyday expressions that come to us from sailing and the sea.

About the Illustrator

Tina Holdcroft was born in Stoke-on-Trent, England, but came to Canada with her parents when she was twelve and has lived in the Toronto area ever since. The illustrator of several children's books, including *Taking Care of Crumley, ScienceWorks, Dr. Z's Magic Mud*, and *The Bop*, her work has appeared in numerous national and international magazines, newspapers, and advertising campaigns.

KEITH MORGAN, TORONTO

Avid sailors, Holdcroft and her husband, Keith Morgan, spent three of the last six years sailing their boat, *Gooseberry*, across the Atlantic and to the Caribbean.